Just Between Friends

Copyright © 1997

Brownlow Publishing Company
6309 Airport Freeway
Fort Worth, Texas 76117

ISBN: 1-57051-160-8

Artwork by Jane Wooster Scott and
provided by Superstock

Cover/Interior:
Koechel Peterson & Associates

Printed in USA

A Special Gift

for:

_____

from:

_____

date:

_____

Anyone with a heart full of friendship
has a hard time finding enemies.

Cherished Moments Gift Books

A Basket of Friends

A Feast of Friendship

Friends of a Feather

Just Between Friends

Leaves of Gold:
An Inspirational Classic for our Time

Merry Christmas With Love

Seeds of Kindness: Garden Thoughts for the Heart

Sweet Rose of Friendship

Tea for Two: Taking Time for Friends

Where Angels Dwell:
A Treasury for Hope, Inspiration and Blessing

Just Between Friends

by Mary Hollingsworth

Brownlow

Selfless Love

The world bows to people who have so committed themselves to each other.

Friendship. There's something so special about that word.

In honor of friendship wars have been fought and won, fortunes have been given away, crowns have been relinquished.

In service to friendship we stand vigil at the bedside of the dying, adopt orphans, care for widows and clothe the needy. Friendship brings warmth to a shivering beggar, company to the lonely and laughter to the hurting.

In commitment to friendship men and women have been burned at the stake, torn apart by lions, maimed, imprisoned and martyred.

In tribute to friendship symphonies have been composed, classics written and masterpieces painted.

It's a word of respect and awe, a word of prayer and hope. It's love in its rarest, most selfless form...friendship.

Anyone with a heart full of friendship
has a hard time finding enemies.

Remember, you're never a failure if you have a friend.
"CLARENCE" IT'S A WONDERFUL LIFE

The thing that counts most in pursuit of happiness
is choosing the right traveling companion.

Two persons will not be friends long,
if they cannot forgive each other's little failings.
LA BRUYERE

Bits and Pieces

Bits and pieces.
Bits and pieces.

People. People important to you. People unimportant to you cross your life, touch it with love and move on. There are people who leave you, and you breathe a sigh of relief and wonder why you ever came in contact with them. There are people who leave you, and you breathe a sigh of remorse and wonder why they had to go and leave such a gaping hole.

Children leave parents. Friends leave friends. Acquaintance move on. People change homes. People grow apart. Enemies hate and move on. Friends love and move on. You think of th

many who have moved into your hazy memory.
You look at those present and wonder.

I believe in God's master plan in lives. He moves people in
and out of each other's lives, and each leaves his mark on
the other. You find you are made up of bits and pieces of all
who ever touched your life, and you are more because of it,
and you would be less if they had not touched you.

Pray God that you accept the bits and pieces in humility,
and wonder, and never question, and never regret.

Bits and pieces.
Bits and pieces.

UNKNOWN

Friendly Forgiveness

Forgiveness is not something we need, you and I,

for I have accepted you as you are, and you me.

You know that I am weak and make mistakes.

I disappoint and hurt you, no doubt.

But at the same instant you know

it is without intention or malice.

And I know the same of you.

Because we have decided to be friends,

we simply forgave each other

once for all time at the beginning.

I thank You, God in heaven, for friends. When morning wakes, when daytime ends, I have the consciousness of loving hands that touch my own, of tender glance and gentle tone, of thoughts that cheer and bless! Amen.

MARGARET SANGSTER

Friends do not live in harmony merely, as some say, but in melody.

HENRY DAVID THOREAU

Friends become our chosen families.

No soul is desolate as long as there is a human being for whom it can feel trust and reverence.

GEORGE ELIOT

One is taught by experience to put a premium on
those few people who can appreciate you for what you are.

GAIL GODWIN

Like everything breathing of kindness
Like these is the love of a friend.

A. P. STANLEY

The ideal of friendship is to feel as one,
while remaining two.

MADAME SWETCHINE

It Takes Two

The desire for friendship is strong
in every human heart. We crave the
companionship of those who understand.
The nostalgia of life presses,
we sigh for "home," and long for the
presence of one who sympathizes
with our aspirations, comprehends our hopes,
and is able to partake of our joys.
A thought is not our own until
we impart it to another,
and the confessional seems to be
a crying need of every human soul.

One can bear grief, but it takes two to be glad.

ELBERT HUBBARD

He covers the sky with clouds; he supplies the earth
with rain and makes grass grow on the hills.

PSALM 147:8

True friendship is a knot which angel hands have tied.

ANONYMOUS

If seeds in the black earth can turn into such
beautiful roses, what might not the heart of man
become in its long journey toward the stars?

G. K. CHESTERTON

Sticking Together

Together we stick; divided we're stuck.
EVON HEDLEY

I have decided to stick with love.
Hate is too great a burden to bear.
MARTIN LUTHER KING, JR.

Yes'm old friends is always best,
'less you can catch a new one that's
fit to make an old one out of.
SARAH ORNE JEWETT

With a friend you can
always be yourself.

True friendship comes when
silence between two people is comfortable.

DAVE TYSON GENTRY

I hold this task to be the highest task for a bond between
two people; that each protects the solitude of the other.

RAINER MARIA RILKE

Silences make the real conversations between friends.
Not the saying but the never needing to say is what counts.

MARGARET LEE RUNBECK

If I mayn't tell you what I feel,
what is the use of a friend?

WILLIAM MAKEPEACE THACKERAY

Eloquent Silence

We don't always have to talk, and I'm glad we're comfortable being quiet together. I draw incredible strength and hope by just being in the same room with you or walking with you through a quiet park. The silence between us says so many things eloquently. It says, "I trust you to understand my mood today." "I'm thankful I don't need to try and impress you with my words." "I love you, and you know it without my always having to say so." "I need to be with you today just be with you."

If you must say something to me today, say it with a smile, a hug or a squeeze of my hand. I'll understand. Some things are better said with silence than with clumsy conversation. Let our silence continue.

Kindred Spirits

The pleasure of your company is a many-sided affair.
It includes the pleasure of seeing you, the pleasure of
hearing you talk, the drama of watching your actions,
your likes and dislikes and adventures; the pleasure of
hunting you up in your haunts, and the delicate flattery
I feel when you hunt me up in mine. I mean all this and
more when I say that I find you congenial. Congeniality,
when once established between two kindred spirits or in a
group, is the most carefree of human relationships. It is
effortless, like purring. It is a basic theme in friendship.

FRANCES LESTER WARNER

A Haphazard Fashion

Friendships do not grow up in any carefully tended and contemplated fashion.... They begin haphazard.

As we look back on the first time we saw our friends we find that generally our original impression was curiously astray. We have worked along beside them, have grown to cherish their delicious absurdities, have outrageously imposed on each other's patience and suddenly we awoke to realize what had happened.

We had, without knowing it, gained a new friend.

CHRISTOPHER MORLEY

Five years from now you will be pretty much the same
as you are today except for two things: the books you read
and the people you get close to.

CHARLES JONES

One loyal friend is worth ten thousand relatives.

EURIPIDES

There are evergreen men and women in the world, praise
be to God! not many of them, but a few. The sun of our
prosperity makes the green of their friendship no brighter,
the frost of our adversity kills not the leaves of their affection.

JEROME K. JEROME

Because you bring me nearer to God, you are my friend.

UNKNOWN

The Wide Horizon

Friendship means sharing interests and this means
widening one's horizon. It involves loving kindness
and patience, never faultfinding or criticism.
Too often I hear people explaining just what their
friends have done wrong. I do not consider this
true friendship! My own dearest friends seem
neither to have faults themselves nor to find them
in others. They seem always to be giving generously
of themselves, without question or pause, and even
the smallest of incidents will remind me of this.

GLADYS TABER

A Lot Like Me

I like myself—I really do. Oh, it's not false pride as much as realizing that usually I'm all I've got. So, I'd rather be with someone I like for the rest of my life than with someone I don't.

Sure, I could be extremely hard on myself because I know my own faults better than anyone else. But the truth is, I'm doing the best I know how with all my heart, and I know it, whether anyone else can tell or not.

I love life and people and my work. And I've struggled hard through the years to be good at what I do. Oh, I know I haven't arrived yet, but I appreciate myself for who I am striving to become.

Sometimes I laugh with myself at myself, and sometimes we cry together. I have to take myself with a grain of salt (and a spoonful of sugar) and hope others will be gracious enough to take me that way, too. I give myself the benefit of the doubt and examine carefully my intent and effort, rather than my actual success or failure, for life is the striving, not just the accomplishment.

Yes, I like me—I admit it. I'm my own best friend. And because I like and accept myself for who and what I am, I can like and accept you as you are. Perhaps that's why I like you so much after all...you're a lot like me.

Friendship with oneself

is all-important

because without it

one cannot be friends with

anyone else in the world.

ELEANOR ROOSEVELT

If I Had Known

If I had known what trouble you were bearing
What griefs were in the silence of your face;
I would have been more gentle, and more caring,
And tried to give you gladness for a space.
I would have brought more warmth into the place,
If I had known.

If I had known what thoughts despairing drew you;
(Why do we never try to understand?)
I would have lent a little friendship to you,
And slipped my hand within your hand,
And made your stay more pleasant in the land,
If I had known.

MARY CAROLYN DAVIES

Two may talk together under the same roof
for many years, yet never really meet;
and two others at first speech are old friends.

MARY CATHERWOOD

Sir, more than kisses, letters mingle souls;
For, thus friends absent speak.

JOHN DONNE

It is good to be attracted out of ourselves,
to be forced to take a near view of the sufferings,
the privations, the efforts, the difficulties of others.

CHARLOTTE BRONTË

And remember, we all stumble, every one of us.
That's why it's a comfort to go hand in hand.

EMILY KIMBROUGH

What joy
is better than
the news
of friends?

ROBERT BROWNING

Comfortably Together

My coat and I live comfortably together. It has
assumed all my wrinkles, does not hurt me anywhere,
has molded itself to my deformities and is complacent to
all my movements. I only feel its presence because it
keeps me warm. Old coats and old friends are the same.

VICTOR HUGO

We do not wish for friends to feed and clothe our
bodies—neighbors are kind enough for that—but
to do the like office for our spirits.

HENRY DAVID THOREAU

Flowers leave a part of their fragrance
in the hands that bestow them.

Old Friendships

Full of tears and warmth is an old friendship
That asks no longer deeds of gallantry,
Or any deed at all—save that the friend shall be
Alive and breathing somewhere, like a song.

EUNICE TIETJENS

A true friend laughs at your stories even when
they're not so good, and sympathizes with your troubles
even when they're not so bad.

PROVERB

Everything we do, dear friends,
is for your strengthening.

2 CORINTHIANS 12:19

Empathy

Empathy is your hurt in my heart. It is your unspoken pain flowing as tears from my eyes. It is my feeling of melancholy today because of your sorrow. And it's that nervous, queasy feeling in the pit of my stomach because you're facing a difficult task.

But empathy is also the song I sing when you're happy. It's the exhilaration and pride I know when you get a standing ovation. It's your joy expressing itself in my laughter. And it's your peace that calms my heart.

Empathy is your soul living in me.

We Only Have Today

Our friendship cannot rely on our past together.
And it cannot rely on the future we anticipate. It must
be now. It must be today. For our past is only precious
memories, and our future is still misty imaginings.
Can't we find time to be together today?

Life is a series of surprises and would not be worth taking
or keeping if it were not. God delights to isolate us every
day and hide from us the past and the future.

RALPH WALDO EMERSON

The language of friendship is not words, but meanings.
It is an intelligence above language.

Friendtuition

Even from across the room I can tell by the pitch of your voice whether you're happy or bored. And the slope of your shoulders says you're discouraged or exhilarated. Your hands let me know if you're nervous or calm. And I can see behind your eyes to your inner joy or pain. Your swinging foot says you are frustrated. And the way you play with your ring helps me guess your preoccupation. Some days you laugh and talk excitedly, but other days you're quiet, tired and pensive.

The mystery of friendship is that two people, though separated by distance, can be so close. It's a kind of *friendtuition*, I believe. The sadness of it all is that two people might sit side by side and yet remain miles apart.

A friend hears the song in my heart
and sings it to me when my memory fails.

A friend will joyfully sing with you when you are on the
mountaintop and silently walk beside you through the valley.

No distance of place or lapse of time can lessen
the friendship of those who are thoroughly persuaded
of each other's worth.

ROBERT SOUTHEY

We are so very rich if we know just a few people
in a way in which we know no others.

CATHERINE BRAMWELL-BOOTH

Knowing You, Knowing Me

You understand what I have left unsaid. You appreciate in me things I have long since taken for granted. You suggest the improvements I need to make for areas of my life I had written off as hopeless. And you challenge me to use talents I deny or help me see when I'm chasing pipe dreams. You call me to higher aspirations than I can imagine for myself and give me courage to try new things. In knowing you, I no longer wonder who I really am because, through you, I see my own dignity, honor and worth. Through you I am able to overcome my feelings of failure and weakness. In you I see a clearer image of me. In knowing you, I know me.

Free to Be Friends

Peace and joy bless the friend
who comes to see and hear and not to change.

In friendship we find nothing false or insincere; everything
is straightforward, and springs from the heart.

CICERO

Meeting you was like suddenly

seeing myself in a mirror.

We were never strangers

you and I—

only friends yet unfound.

The greatest gift we can give one another
is rapt attention to one another's existence.

SUE ATCHLEY EBAUGH

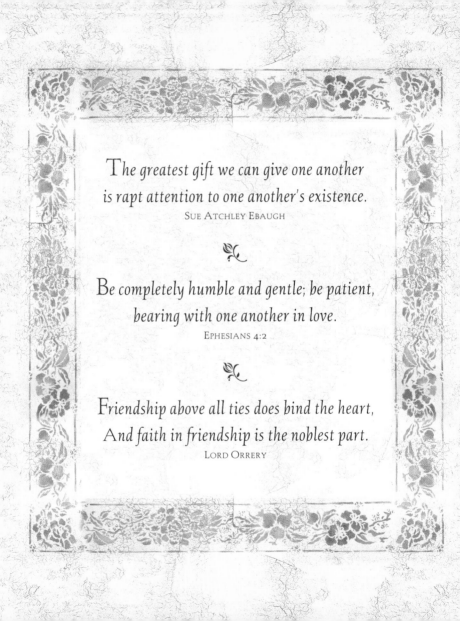

Be completely humble and gentle; be patient,
bearing with one another in love.

EPHESIANS 4:2

Friendship above all ties does bind the heart,
And faith in friendship is the noblest part.

LORD ORRERY

If we would build on a sure foundation
in friendship, we must love our friends for
their sakes rather than for our *own;*
we must look at their truth to *themselves* full
as much —as their truth to us.

CHARLOTTE BRONTË

Treat your friends for what you know them
to be. Regard no surfaces, consider not what
they did, but what they intended.

HENRY DAVID THOREAU

Friends of the Heart

I don't want to be just another friend that tugs away at you for your precious time, your attention and your love. I want to be someone you come to for understanding, someone to whom you retreat for emotional rest. I want to be someone with whom you can laugh and share your joy, one on whose shoulder you can cry without embarrassment or apology and one whose hand you can reach for when you need comfort or support.

I want you to be able to say to me,

"I feel lonely today; stay with me a while longer."

Or, "Can you come over? I need to talk to you."

I just want to be there for you, as you so often are for me.

I want us to be friends of the heart.

Because You Are My Friend

I wish you the courage to be warm when the world
would prefer that you be cool.
I wish you success sufficient to your needs;
I wish you failure to temper that success.
I wish you joy in all your days;
I wish you sadness so that you may better measure joy.
I wish you gladness to overbalance grief.
I wish you humor and a twinkle in the eye.
I wish you glory and the strength to bear its burdens.
I wish you sunshine on your path and storms
to season your journey.
I wish you peace—in the world in which you live and in the
smallest corner of the heart where truth is kept.
I wish you faith—to help define your living and your life.
More I cannot wish you—except perhaps love—
to make all the rest worthwhile.

ROBERT A. WARD

At the heart of love there is a simple secret:
the lover lets the beloved be free.

UNKNOWN

There is a wonderful, mystical law of nature
that the three things we crave most in life—happiness,
freedom, and peace of mind—are always attained
by giving them to someone else.

UNKNOWN

For it was a spiritual joy;
my soul knew that here was a soul that would
understand and be in harmony with mine.

TERESA OF AVILA

And when we come to think of it,
goodness is uneventful. It does not flash, it glows.
It is deep, quiet, and very simple.
It may be felt in the touch of a friendly hand
or the look of a kindly eye.

DAVID GRAYSON

Life is a chronicle of friendship. Friends create the
world anew each day. Without their loving care,
courage would not suffice to keep hearts strong for life.

HELEN KELLER

Every part is disposed to unite with the whole,
that it may thereby escape from its incompleteness.

LEONARDO DA VINCI

Friendship is like two clocks keeping time.

ANONYMOUS

A truly faithful friend is the medicine of life; a truly
faithful friend, a strong covering. For what would not a
genuine friend do? What pleasure would he not create for us?
What profit? What safety? Though thou were to name a
thousand treasures, there is nothing comparable to a real friend.

ARETHUSA TO ST. JOHN

To like and dislike the same things,
that is indeed true friendship.

SALLUST

Better one true friend than a hundred acquaintances.

EARLY AMERICAN PROVERB

Small Pleasures

If all could realize the power of even a small pleasure, how much happier the world would be! And how much longer bodies and souls both would bear up under living! Sensitive people realize that often it happens to them to be revived, kindled, strengthened to a degree which they could not describe, by some little thing—some word of praise, some token of remembrance, some proof of affection or recognition.

HELEN HUNT JACKSON

The Hearts Anchor

Think of me as your friend, I pray,
And call me by a loving name;
I will not care what others say,
If only you remain the same.
I will not care how dark the night,
I will not care how wild the storm,
Your love will fill my heart with light
And shield me close and keep me warm

Think of me as your friend, I pray,
For else my life is little worth:
So shall your memory light my way,
Although we meet no more on earth.
For while I know your faith secure,
I ask no happier fate to see:
Thus to be loved by one so pure
Is honor rich enough for me.

WILLIAM WINTER

Sweet Recognition

When we first met, you smiled warmly.
It was a welcome and polite smile that
extended friendship, and I knew I wanted
to see it again. Time and togetherness spread
that beautiful smile into your eyes, and
they would twinkle happily when you saw
me. Now, when I catch your eye, I can tell
we have come to know each other very well.
Your whole face lights up in sweet
recognition. But I'm sure the light in
your face is only a reflection of the smile
on mine at that same moment.

True Friendship

My heart has just been called back to the time
when we used to sit with our arms around each
other at the sunset hour & talk & talk of our
friends & our homes & of ten thousand subjects of
mutual interest until both our hearts felt warmer
and lighter for the pure communion of spirit.

ANTOINETTE LOUISA BROWN